The secret of a successful Entrepreneur: A road map to success

Tables of contents

Who is an entrepreneur?

An entrepreneur is someone who creates and manages their own company or business, frequently taking on financial risk in the process.

Entrepreneurs frequently come up with novel or original ideas and are prepared to face difficulties and unknowns to realise their goals. They may be motivated by a variety of things, including monetary gain, personal fulfilment, or a desire to bring about societal change, but they are frequently driven by a desire to achieve and to have a beneficial impact on the world.

Successful business owners are those who have founded and expanded organisations that have made a substantial contribution to society or the economy. These people frequently have a high level of motivation, are creative, and are willing to take calculated risks to succeed.

Types of entrepreneur

There are several types of entrepreneurs, including:

Small Business Entrepreneurs: These are individuals who start and run small businesses to make a profit.

Social Entrepreneurs: These entrepreneurs aim to solve social or environmental issues by creating and implementing innovative solutions.

Serial Entrepreneurs: These are entrepreneurs who have started and successfully run multiple businesses over time.

Lifestyle Entrepreneurs: These entrepreneurs aim to create a business that supports their desired lifestyle, rather than making profit their primary goal.

Scalable Start-Up Entrepreneurs: These entrepreneurs create and grow businesses with the goal of rapid growth and scaling to a large size.

Innovative Entrepreneurs: These entrepreneurs are focused on creating new products or services that disrupt the market and offer unique value to customers.

Freelance Entrepreneurs: These are self-employed individuals who offer their services on a project basis, such as writers, designers, or consultants

Tech Entrepreneurs: These entrepreneurs focus on creating and developing new technology-based products or services.

Corporate Entrepreneurs: These are entrepreneurs who work within established companies, but have the mindset and skills of an entrepreneur to innovate and develop new products, services or business models within the company.

Keys to Business Success

Entrepreneurs frequently experience great success, which is one of their habits.

Vision: Successful business people have a distinct idea of their goals and how they intend to attain them.

Flexibility: They can modify their business approach in response to changing conditions.
They can recover from failures and setbacks and keep working toward their objectives. When things don't go as planned, they may adapt and change their strategy because they view failure as an opportunity to learn.

Creativity: Successful Entrepreneurs are frequently very creative and capable of developing novel solutions to issues.

Focus: They can maintain their concentration on their objectives and set priorities for their time and resources.

Persistence: Successful business people are tenacious and persistent, and they are prepared to work hard to accomplish their objectives.

Risk-taking: They are prepared to take calculated risks to accomplish their objectives, but they also have the skills to manage and reduce such risks.
Leadership: Strong leaders who can inspire and motivate their people to succeed are frequently successful entrepreneurs.

In general, being a successful entrepreneur needs a mix of abilities, characteristics, and behaviours that enable people to recognize and seize opportunities, control risk, and generate value for their stakeholders and themselves.

They are motivated and focused because of their enthusiasm for their company and their goal.

Entrepreneurs who are successful frequently innovate. They continually seek out new and improved methods of doing things and are not hesitant to take chances while attempting anything novel.

They are adept at prioritising things and managing their time well. They can strike a balance between conflicting demands and maintain attention to what matters most.

Successful entrepreneurs are lifelong learners. They have an insatiable desire to learn new things and develop their talents and are open-minded and curious by nature.

They are aware of the value of networking and establishing contacts. They are adept at establishing and sustaining relationships over time and can connect with others who can assist them in achieving their objectives.

Self-control: They possess self-control and positive behaviours. Even when they don't feel like it, they can remain productive and focused while avoiding distractions and staying on track.

The basic idea of Entrepreneurship.

The basic idea of entrepreneurship is to identify a need in the market or a problem that needs to be solved, and then to create a product, service, or solution that addresses that need or problem.

Entrepreneurs often start with an idea, which they develop into a business plan. The business plan outlines the vision for the business, the target market, the competition, the marketing strategy, the financial projections, and other important details.

Once the business plan is in place, the entrepreneur must secure the necessary funding and resources to launch the business. This may involve borrowing money, seeking investors, or using personal savings. The entrepreneur then begins to build the team, develop the product or service, and launch the business.

Entrepreneurship is not just about starting a new business, it is also about innovation and creating value. Entrepreneurs are often motivated by a desire to make a difference in the world, solve a problem, or create something new and innovative. They must be willing to take risks, work hard, and persevere through challenges.

Successful entrepreneurs are often characterised by their creativity, vision, determination, and willingness to learn from failure. They can adapt to changing market conditions, take calculated risks, and seize opportunities when they arise.

In summary, the basic idea of entrepreneurship is to identify a need or problem in the market, create a product or service that addresses that need or problem, and then launch a new business to bring that product or service to market. It requires creativity, vision, determination, and a willingness to take risks and learn from failure.

How successful entrepreneurs overcome failure

Entrepreneurs can start businesses in a range of industries, including technology, finance, food, and retail. They come from varied backgrounds. Some business owners start as solo operations, while others build teams and expand their businesses to achieve greater success. Furthermore, failure is an essential part of the process. In actuality, many of the most prosperous businesses in history had to overcome significant barriers before succeeding.

So, how can savvy business people recover from setbacks? These are some strategies that have been successful in the past:
Perceive failure as an opportunity to learn: Successful businesses view failure as a learning experience rather than a setback. They analyse their mistakes, ascertain what went wrong, and

then use that knowledge to inform decisions going forward.

Maintain an optimistic outlook: Successful business people remain upbeat despite failure. They are aware that setbacks are temporary and that, with a continued commitment to their objectives, success is attainable.

Adapt to change: Successful Entrepreneurs do not hesitate to alter their business model or strategy in the event of failure. They understand that change is necessary for progress, thus they are willing to take risks to achieve their goals.

Get guidance and assistance: Entrepreneurs that have failed typically look to peers, advisers, and/or peers for mentorship and support. They are aware of the value of consulting individuals who have overcome similar challenges and may offer insight.

Be persistent; successful businesses do not easily give up. They understand that building a successful business takes time, persistence, and work. They remain committed to their goals and make a lot of effort even in the face of setbacks.

Important of networking

Access to resources: Through networking, business owners can develop connections with other professionals in their area, which may result in the exchange of practical resources like information, contacts, and tools. Buyers can find the products they need to sell on Amazon by using networking to connect with suppliers, producers, and other sellers.

Opportunities for cooperation might arise from networking, allowing business owners to collaborate on initiatives or projects. This may mean cooperating with other vendors to package products, create team-based promotions, or trade data and resources.

Feedback and Help: Networking may provide entrepreneurs with constructive criticism and assistance. Other professionals might offer insights and opinions on their business goals, products, and marketing initiatives. Businesses may improve their customer service, listing quality, and pricing strategies with the help of this customer feedback.

Business entrepreneurs can establish their brands and establish themselves as authorities in their professions by networking. As a result, businesspeople might become more well-known and credible, which might encourage more customers to buy from them and increase sales.

Growth opportunities: Networking can present business owners with prospects for growth and development. Shoppers can learn about new markets, goods, and business strategies that may help them develop their company by networking with other professionals in their industry.

How successful entrepreneur identify market Gaps

Identifying a speciality is an important step in creating a successful business. and it is a skill that very effective business people excel at. Finding a market gap essentially entails locating a segment of the market that is underserved by already available goods or services and producing something to fill that void.

When spotting market gaps, successful business people frequently follow these steps:
Market research: When launching a firm, successful entrepreneurs do their homework. They do in-depth market research to determine

what goods or services are being offered, the level of demand, and any gaps that could be filled.

Find client pain points: Entrepreneurs frequently search for areas where customers are having issues or are frustrated. They then develop remedies to deal with such problems.

Analyse trends: Entrepreneurs keep abreast of current trends and employ their knowledge to spot possible market gaps. For instance, they might see a rise in demand for organic foods and decide to start a company that sells a variety of organic goods.

Identify market gaps by drawing on personal experience. Entrepreneurs frequently do this. For instance, customers might decide to design the product themselves if they are having problems finding a certain kind of item.

Customers' opinions matter, thus successful business people pay close attention to them and use them to enhance their goods and services. Based on client ideas or grievances, they could potentially spot market gaps.

Building a strong team

Any business owner who wants to create a successful company must first assemble a solid staff. Entrepreneurs may scale their business over time, manage day-to-day operations, and realise their vision with the aid of a solid team.

These are some crucial actions a businessperson can take to assemble a capable team:

Clearly outline the functions and responsibilities of each position before recruiting anyone. Entrepreneurs should do this before hiring anyone. This makes it possible to guarantee that the proper people are employed for the right positions.

Hire for skills and cultural fit: Entrepreneurs should seek out new team members who not only possess the required knowledge and abilities but also have a strong sense of the company's culture. To foster a supportive and cooperative work environment, cultural compatibility is crucial.

Maintaining a successful team needs a commitment to continuous training and development. Entrepreneurs should support their staff members' professional development and give them the tools they need to be successful.

Encourage open communication: Effective teamwork depends on open communication. Entrepreneurs should promote open communication among their staff members by creating a secure and encouraging work atmosphere.

Provide clear goals and expectations: By creating clear goals and expectations, the team may more effectively work together toward a common goal. The team's leaders should establish clear objectives for themselves and hold each other accountable for achieving them.

Recognize and acknowledge accomplishments: Business owners should commend and honour their teams' hard work. This can take the shape of incentives like bonuses, raises, or other types of recognition that let team members know their efforts and contributions are valued.

Encourage a good and inclusive work environment: A strong team requires a positive and inclusive work environment. Entrepreneurs should foster an environment where everyone feels respected and supported and where there is respect for all people.

Collaboration

Although working together might make entrepreneurship easier and more successful, it can also be a difficult journey. For several reasons, collaboration is crucial for business owners. Entrepreneurs can first take advantage of the skills and strengths of others. It's easy for entrepreneurs to become engrossed in their vision and ideas, but working together can lead to new insights, perspectives, and ideas that you would not have had previously. You may be able to fill in any knowledge or skill gaps you may have with the assistance of others' expertise .

Second, cooperation can result in increased effectiveness and efficiency. Entrepreneurs can do more by collaborating and pooling resources than they could on their own. For instance, when two business owners work together, they might develop a more comprehensive good or service that appeals to a larger clientele. Collaboration can also assist business owners to divide their effort and lower their risk of burnout.

Finally, working together can improve the chances of success. When business owners collaborate, they can split the costs and risks of launching a new company. Finding funds, breaking into new markets, and overcoming obstacles may all be made simpler as a result. Collaboration can also help you reach new audiences and improve the visibility of your business.

How successful entrepreneurs turn Ideas into profitable businesses

The first stage in developing an idea into a successful business is to investigate the market and validate your concept. This entails knowing your target market, pinpointing their requirements and problems, and confirming that there is a market for your goods or service.

Create a Business Plan: After you have tested your idea, it is crucial to put together a thorough business plan that details your objectives, company plans, and financial projections.

projections. As you try to develop your idea into a successful business, this will assist you in remaining focused and on course.

Create a Powerful Team: Successful business owners are aware that they cannot accomplish everything alone. To transform your idea into a successful business, you must first assemble a solid team of collaborators, mentors, and advisers. Seek people who can assist you in realising your idea and who have similar visions to yours.

Make a Prototype: If you're working on a physical product, it's crucial to make a prototype to test your ideas and find any potential problems. You may use this to improve your product and make sure that it satisfies the needs of your target market.

Once your product or service has been established, it's time to launch your company and begin bringing in money. Successful business people understand that there is still work to be done. They make enhancements and adjustments to their product or service based on client input and market demand to maintain the profitability and success of their company.

Having a good marketing and sales strategy is a requisite for a successful entrepreneur. This entails developing a brand, identifying the target audience, and using a variety of channels to connect with them and turn them into paying clients.

A simplified version of the product or service should be created as a minimum viable product (MVP) by the entrepreneur. The market should test the MVP to get input and confirm the business plan's presumptions.

Mitigating Business Risk

You can use a variety of tactics as an entrepreneur to reduce business risks, and they are quite effective.

Perform in-depth market research: Market research is essential before launching a new product or service to identify demand, rivalry, and possible profitability. You'll be able to recognize potential hazards and make wise decisions as a result.

Increase the variety of goods and services you offer. A company that only offers one good or service is more susceptible to changes in the market and competition. By diversifying your products, you can reduce risk and protect yourself from market changes.

Have a strong brand and reputation: Having a strong brand and reputation can help you attract repeat business, which can keep your business afloat even in difficult economic times. Also, it might help you stand out from other businesses and win over more devoted clients.

Effective financial management is essential for reducing the risks that your company faces. This entails keeping precise financial records, making a budget, and keeping an eye on cash flow. Also, you ought to have a backup plan in place in case of unforeseen circumstances. Have a crisis management plan: It's critical to have a strategy in place for dealing with unforeseen emergencies, including a natural disaster, cyberattack, or public health issue. This can assist you in reacting as fast and effectively as possible, minimising harm to your company.

Establish strong connections with partners and suppliers: Having solid connections with partners and suppliers can help you bargain for lower costs, find trustworthy providers of goods or raw materials, and open up new markets. This may act as a cushion against market turbulence and interruptions.

Continually enhancing your goods or services might aid in maintaining a competitive edge, luring new clients, and boosting sales.

Balancing work and Life

Maintaining a healthy work-life balance can be extremely difficult for entrepreneurs. Entrepreneurs frequently put in long hours and juggle a variety of jobs, including running their companies, selling their goods and services, connecting with customers and partners, and managing administrative duties. They might also have responsibilities to their families and personal lives that need their attention.

Everybody needs to strike a healthy work-life balance, but entrepreneurs need to do it the most. You certainly put a lot of effort and dedication into running your firm as an entrepreneur. On the other hand, neglecting your personal life can have negative effects on both your mental and physical health, resulting in fatigue, stress, and even life-threatening medical conditions.

some tips on how to balance work and life as an entrepreneur:

Establish limits: It's critical to establish boundaries between your personal and professional lives. This could entail setting apart certain work hours as well as time for leisure pursuits like exercise, hobbies, and socialising with loved ones.

Prioritise your tasks: Time management success depends on effective task prioritisation. Decide which chores are most crucial, and concentrate on finishing them first. To save time, think about assigning work to others or outsourcing some duties.

Take advantage of technology: There are a variety of tools and applications that can aid in time management and organisation for business owners. Use time-saving solutions like scheduling apps, project management programs, and social media management systems.

Exercise self-care: It's critical for business owners to look after their physical and emotional well-being. Make time for self-care activities like yoga or meditation as well as regular exercise and a good diet. This may lessen stress and enhance general well-being.

Seek assistance: To manage work and personal life, entrepreneurs can turn to their friends, family, and coworkers for support. Other beneficial materials can be obtained by participating in networking groups, going to industry events, or networking with other business owners.

Cultivate a winning attitude

Stay disciplined and committed: Cultivating a winning attitude requires discipline and commitment. Stay focused on your goals, and be willing to put in the hard work and effort required to achieve them
.

Learn from mistakes: Everyone makes mistakes, but the most successful people use their mistakes as opportunities to learn and grow. Instead of dwelling on failures, use them as opportunities to improve and become better.

Celebrate small victories: Celebrating small victories along the way can help keep you motivated and focused on your goals. Recognize and celebrate your progress, no matter how small it may seem.

Creating a culture for innovation

A winning attitude is crucial for achieving success in any area of life, whether it's in business, sports, or personal relationships. Cultivating a winning attitude requires a combination of mental toughness, self-belief, and a willingness to learn and improve.

Set goals and have a clear vision: To cultivate a winning attitude, you need to have a clear idea of what you want to achieve. Set goals that are challenging but achievable, and create a vision for what you want to accomplish.

Creating a culture of innovation is critical for companies that want to stay competitive and relevant in today's fast-paced business environment. A culture of innovation encourages employees to think outside the box, experiment with new ideas, and take calculated risks to develop new products, services, and business models.

Encourage Creativity and Experimentation: One of the critical elements of creating a culture of innovation is to encourage creativity and experimentation. Employees should feel comfortable exploring new ideas and thinking outside the box. Leaders should provide an environment that fosters creativity and encourages experimentation. For example, companies could set aside time for brainstorming sessions, hackathons, or other activities that encourage employees to come up with new ideas.

Empower Employees: Empowering employees is another critical element of creating a culture of innovation. When employees feel empowered, they are more likely to take ownership of their work and experiment with new ideas. Leaders should provide employees with the resources they need to be successful, such as training, tools, and autonomy.

Celebrate Failure: Failure is an inevitable part of the innovation process. Companies that create a culture of innovation understand that failure is a learning opportunity and should be celebrated. Leaders should encourage employees to take calculated risks and learn from their failures. This approach will help create an environment where employees feel free to experiment and take risks without the fear of negative consequences.

Promote Collaboration: Collaboration is essential for creating a culture of innovation. When employees from different departments and backgrounds work together, they bring different perspectives and expertise to the table, which can lead to new and innovative ideas. Leaders should encourage collaboration by creating cross-functional teams, hosting workshops or events, and providing tools that facilitate collaboration.

Create a Safe Environment: Creating a safe environment is critical for fostering a culture of innovation. Employees should feel comfortable sharing their ideas, even if they are unconventional or risky. Leaders should create an environment where employees feel free to express themselves without fear of judgement or retribution

Why inclusivity matters in business

Because it promotes collaboration, encourages innovation and creativity, and enhances decision-making, inclusivity is essential in business. Businesses that respect diversity foster a workplace where varied viewpoints, experiences, and backgrounds are valued. This enables a wide range of thoughts and strategies to be taken into account, which may result in better answers and more fruitful outcomes.

In addition, customers and clients now want inclusiveness and community representation from enterprises. Businesses that don't value diversity run the danger of alienating current and potential customers, but those that do can gain a competitive edge.

To bridge the opportunity gap for underrepresented groups including women, minorities, and those from low-income backgrounds, inclusivity in entrepreneurship must also be promoted. Entrepreneurs from all backgrounds can expand and build their enterprises, creating more chances for themselves and others, by giving these groups access to resources and support, such as mentorship, networking opportunities, and investment.

Developing a winning business plan

Developing a winning business plan is crucial for any entrepreneur who wants to succeed in their business. A business plan is a roadmap that outlines your business goals, strategies, and tactics. It provides a blueprint for your business's success and is essential for securing funding from investors or loans from financial institutions

Define your business idea and market: The first step in developing a winning business plan is to define your business idea and market. This involves researching the market to identify potential customers, competition, and trends. You should also identify your target audience and develop a unique value proposition that sets your business apart from competitors.

Set realistic goals and objectives: Your business plan should include specific and realistic goals and objectives. These should be measurable and attainable, and you should develop a plan to achieve them.

Stay flexible and adapt: A winning business plan is not a static document. You should be willing to adapt and make changes as your business grows and evolves. Stay open to new opportunities and be willing to pivot your strategy as needed.

www.ingramcontent.com/pod-product-compliance
Lightning Source LLC
Chambersburg PA
CBHW071145220526
45467CB00015B/1977